EXPLORING THE STATES

Nevada

THE BATTLE BORN STATE

by Blake Hoena

BELLWETHER MEDIA · MINNEAPOLIS, MN

Note to Librarians, Teachers, and Parents:

Blastoff! Readers are carefully developed by literacy experts and combine standards-based content with developmentally appropriate text.

Level 1 provides the most support through repetition of high-frequency words, light text, predictable sentence patterns, and strong visual support.

Level 2 offers early readers a bit more challenge through varied simple sentences, increased text load, and less repetition of high-frequency words.

Level 3 advances early-fluent readers toward fluency through increased text and concept load, less reliance on visuals, longer sentences, and more literary language.

Level 4 builds reading stamina by providing more text per page, increased use of punctuation, greater variation in sentence patterns, and increasingly challenging vocabulary.

Level 5 encourages children to move from "learning to read" to "reading to learn" by providing even more text, varied writing styles, and less familiar topics.

Whichever book is right for your reader, Blastoff! Readers are the perfect books to build confidence and encourage a love of reading that will last a lifetime!

This edition first published in 2014 by Bellwether Media, Inc.

No part of this publication may be reproduced in whole or in part without written permission of the publisher. For information regarding permission, write to Bellwether Media, Inc., Attention: Permissions Department, 5357 Penn Avenue South, Minneapolis, MN 55419.

Library of Congress Cataloging-in-Publication Data

Hoena, B. A.
 Nevada / by Blake Hoena.
   pages cm. – (Blastoff! readers. Exploring the states)
 Includes bibliographical references and index.
 Summary: "Developed by literacy experts for students in grades three through seven, this book introduces young readers to the geography and culture of Nevada"–Provided by publisher.
 ISBN 978-1-62617-027-8 (hardcover : alk. paper)
 1. Nevada–Juvenile literature. I. Title.
 F841.3.H64 2014
 979.3–dc23
                                                              2013007777

Printed in the United States of America, North Mankato, MN.

Table of Contents

Where Is Nevada?

Nevada is located in the southwestern United States. Its capital, Carson City, sits near the state's western border with California. Oregon and Idaho lie north of Nevada. Utah and Arizona are its neighbors to the east.

The Sierra Nevada mountain range towers over western Nevada. The rest of the state lies in the Great **Basin**. This is a dry region of mountains and valleys between the Sierra Nevada and Rocky Mountains. Nevada is the seventh largest state.

Pacific Ocean

Oregon

Idaho

Pyramid
Lake

● Reno

⭐ Carson City

Nevada

Utah

California

Las Vegas
●
●
Henderson

Did you know?

Nevada comes from a Spanish
word that means "snow-covered."
The snow-capped Sierra Nevada
earned the state its name.

Arizona

Nevada's largest groups of **Native** Americans were the Paiute, Shoshone, and Washoe. Europeans began exploring the area in the late 1700s. The region was claimed by Spain first and Mexico later. The United States took control of Nevada in 1848. Nevada became a state during the **Civil War**. This earned it the nickname "The Battle Born State."

Shoshone Tribe

Nevada Timeline!

1776: Francisco Garcés of Spain is perhaps the first European to visit Nevada.

1821: Mexico takes control of Nevada from Spain.

1840s: Kit Carson helps explore and map parts of Nevada.

1848: The United States wins Nevada from Mexico after the Mexican-American War.

1859: Gold and silver are discovered near Carson City.

1864: Nevada becomes the thirty-sixth state.

1931: Governor Fred Balzar signs a law that makes casino gambling legal in Nevada.

1936: Construction of the Hoover Dam is complete.

Kit Carson

Mexican-American War

Hoover Dam

The Land

Most of Nevada rests within the Great Basin. This hot, dry region stretches south from Oregon into California, Nevada, and Utah. The Great Basin contains more than 100 small mountain ranges. Between their slopes lie dry grasslands, sandy deserts, and lakes.

The northeastern corner of Nevada is part of a high **plains** area called the Columbia **Plateau**. The granite peaks of the Sierra Nevada line Nevada's western border. The sands of the Mojave Desert cover the state's southern tip. Nevada is the nation's driest state. An average of only 9 inches (23 centimeters) of rain and snow fall each year.

fun fact

The hottest recorded temperature in Nevada was 125 degrees Fahrenheit (52 degrees Celsius). At that temperature, an egg can be cooked in about 20 minutes!

Mojave Desert

Nevada's Climate
average °F

spring
Low: 36°
High: 65°

summer
Low: 53°
High: 90°

fall
Low: 36°
High: 68°

winter
Low: 22°
High: 47°

Pyramid Lake

Thousands of years ago, water covered much of Nevada. Lake Lahontan filled a large part of the Great Basin. What remains of that ancient body of water is now called Pyramid Lake. The lake was named for the pyramid-shaped rocks that rise from its surface.

cui-ui

fun fact

The cui-ui is one of Earth's most ancient species. This rare fish can only be found in Pyramid Lake.

Pyramid Lake is one of the largest natural lakes in Nevada. People enjoy kayaking and fishing in its waters. They also visit the nearby Pyramid Lake Paiute Tribe Museum. Pyramid Lake lies within the Paiute **reservation**. The tribe views it as **sacred**.

Wildlife

Nevada is known for its desert wildlife. Sagebrush covers large portions of the state. Flowering cactuses and yucca plants color the land. Forests cover only a small part of Nevada. **Evergreen trees** grow along the state's mountain slopes.

Nevada's state reptile is the desert tortoise. It munches on plants in southern Nevada. Snakes and lizards also move about the dry landscape. Roadrunners and burrowing owls are common desert birds. Mule deer and bighorn sheep graze on shrubs and grasses. Herds of wild horses and **burros** also roam Nevada.

yucca plant

desert tortoise

burros

Did you know?
Spanish explorers brought horses with them to Nevada. Some of those horses escaped and formed herds. They are the ancestors of the wild horses that now range throughout the state.

wild horses

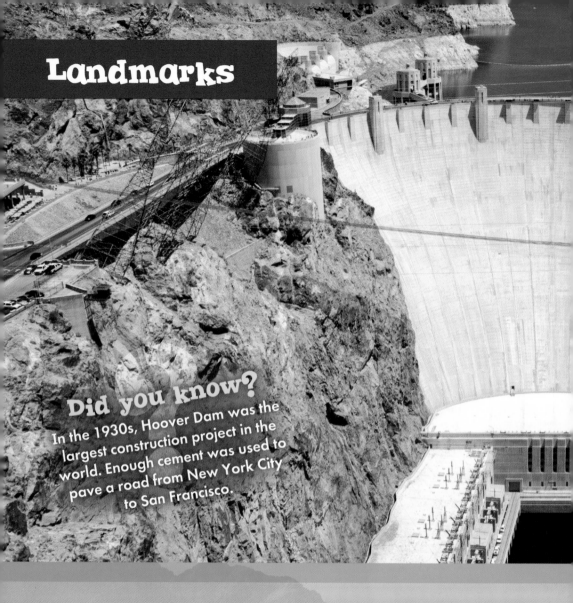

Landmarks

Did you know?
In the 1930s, Hoover Dam was the largest construction project in the world. Enough cement was used to pave a road from New York City to San Francisco.

Each year, more than a million people tour the Hoover **Dam**. This giant barrier spans the Colorado River between Arizona and Nevada. It provides electricity to around 1.3 million people. Close by is the Las Vegas Strip. People visit this famous stretch of road to see shows, go to **casinos**, and take in the dazzling lights.

Hoover Dam

Las Vegas Strip

petroglyphs

East of Las Vegas are
the stunning red rocks of
Gold Butte. The ancient Puebloan people scratched
petroglyphs into the rock walls here. The images are
believed to tell stories of their lives.

Carson City is named after Kit Carson. In the 1840s, Carson helped map and explore stretches of northern Nevada. Carson City was founded in 1858. It was named the state capital when Nevada became a state in 1864.

In 1859, miners discovered silver and gold in the area. Carson City became a **boomtown** as people flocked to its dusty streets. Hotels sprang up, and railroad tracks were laid. In its early years, Carson City was a rough and **lawless** mining town. Today, **tourists** stop in the historic city on their way to Lake Tahoe.

Kit Carson

Working

Did you know?

Nearly three out of every four Nevadans live and work in Clark County. This is where Las Vegas is located.

About one third of all working Nevadans have **service jobs**. They serve the nearly 50 million tourists who visit the state each year. Most of them work in the casinos, hotels, and restaurants of Las Vegas and Reno.

Mining and farming are also important to Nevada. More gold is mined here than in any other state. Only Alaska produces more silver. Nevada has large grasslands that are perfect for grazing cattle and sheep. Farmers grow hay and alfalfa to feed the large herds of livestock.

Where People Work in Nevada

manufacturing
3%

farming and
natural resources
2%

government
11%

services
84%

Playing

Nevada's vast tracks of open land are perfect for outdoor activities. People hike and bike through stretches of wilderness. Downhill skiers enjoy the snowy slopes of the Sierra Nevada Mountains. Hunters target big **game** such as elk and mule deer. Fishers head to lakes to reel in trout and bass.

Nevada's history is rooted in the Wild West. Horseback riding is still popular in the state. Dozens of **rodeos** are held throughout year. Cowboys and cowgirls perform in **lassoing** and riding competitions at these events.

fun fact !

The Reno Rodeo is called the "wildest, richest rodeo in the West!" More than 100,000 fans watch cowboys and cowgirls compete in this 10-day event.

Sheepherder Chili

Ingredients:

3 pounds ground beef

4 tablespoons dried onions

1/4 cup chili powder

1 tablespoon cumin

2 tablespoons Worcestershire sauce

1 teaspoon garlic powder

1/4 teaspoon cayenne pepper

1 teaspoon oregano

1 teaspoon vinegar

1 can stewed tomatoes

1 can tomato sauce

Salt to taste

Black pepper to taste

Water as necessary

Directions:

1. Brown the ground beef in a heavy pot. Drain off the fat and add all the other ingredients.

2. Simmer for at least 2 hours, adding water as needed.

3. Thicken with flour if desired. Serve over rice.

buffet

Did you know?
At one point, the Hilton Hotel in Las Vegas boasted the world's largest buffet. It offered some 500 dishes, including more than 100 desserts!

jerky

Cowboys on the Nevada range would eat thick stews and sourdough bread after long days of work. This kind of hearty Western meal is still enjoyed today. **Jerky**, hamburgers, and steak are popular because of all the cattle raised in the state. Mexican-style dishes with spicy peppers and beans are also common.

Las Vegas is believed to be the birthplace of the all-you-can-eat buffet. In the 1940s, businessman Herb McDonald wanted to attract people to his casino. He offered guests a wide variety of cheap food. They could eat as much as they wanted for one low price. Today, all-you-can-eat buffets are found throughout the United States.

Great Reno
Balloon Race

Every year, the Great Reno Balloon Race draws more than 100,000 spectators. As many as 100 hot air balloons color the Reno skies during this event. Genoa holds the Cowboy Poetry and Music Festival. People here celebrate Nevada's ranching past with words and music.

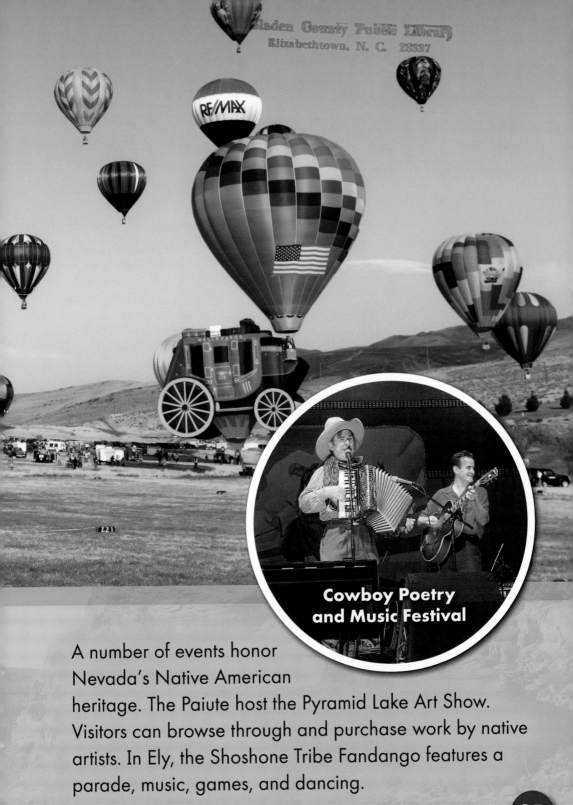

Cowboy Poetry
and Music Festival

A number of events honor
Nevada's Native American
heritage. The Paiute host the Pyramid Lake Art Show.
Visitors can browse through and purchase work by native
artists. In Ely, the Shoshone Tribe Fandango features a
parade, music, games, and dancing.

The Basque

Basque Festival

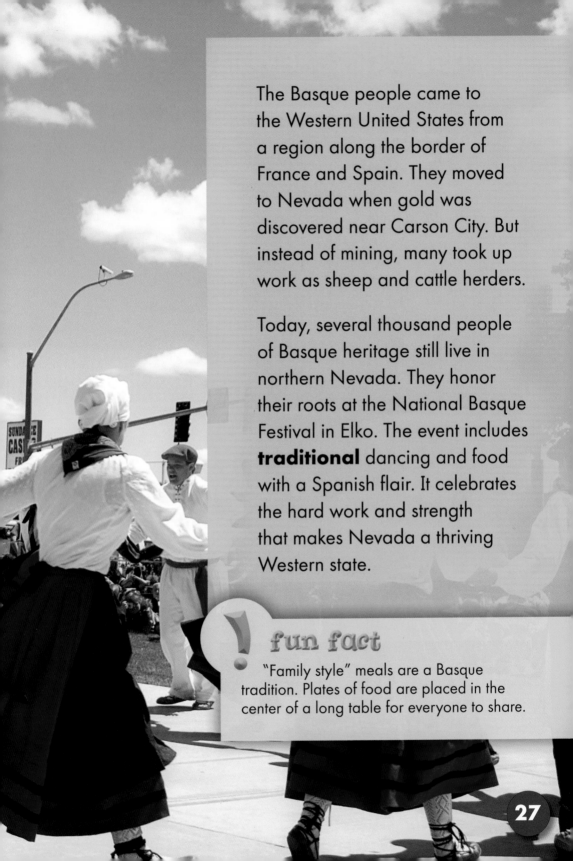

The Basque people came to the Western United States from a region along the border of France and Spain. They moved to Nevada when gold was discovered near Carson City. But instead of mining, many took up work as sheep and cattle herders.

Today, several thousand people of Basque heritage still live in northern Nevada. They honor their roots at the National Basque Festival in Elko. The event includes **traditional** dancing and food with a Spanish flair. It celebrates the hard work and strength that makes Nevada a thriving Western state.

fun fact

"Family style" meals are a Basque tradition. Plates of food are placed in the center of a long table for everyone to share.

Fast Facts About Nevada

Nevada's Flag

Nevada's flag has a solid blue background. Across the upper left corner are the words "Battle Born." Below them sits a single silver star, which represents Nevada's state mineral. Under the star is the word *Nevada*. Framing the state name are two branches of sagebrush, the state flower.

State Flower
sagebrush

State Nicknames:	The Battle Born State
	The Silver State
	The Sagebrush State
State Motto:	"All For Our Country"
Year of Statehood:	1864
Capital City:	Carson City
Other Major Cities:	Las Vegas, Henderson, Reno
Population:	2,700,551 (2010)
Area:	110,572 square miles (286,380 square kilometers); Nevada is the 7th largest state.
Major Industries:	tourism, mining, farming
Natural Resources:	gold, silver
State Government:	42 representatives; 21 senators
Federal Government:	4 representatives; 2 senators
Electoral Votes:	6

State Animal
desert bighorn sheep

State Bird
mountain bluebird

Glossary

basin—an area of land that lies lower than the surrounding land

boomtown—a town that experiences a sudden increase in population

burros—small donkeys

casinos—buildings where people bet money on games of chance

Civil War—a war between the northern (Union) and southern (Confederate) states that lasted from 1861 to 1865

dam—a structure that blocks the flow of water in a river

evergreen trees—trees that stay green and do not lose their leaves in winter

game—wild animals hunted for food or sport

jerky—dried meat

lassoing—using rope with a loop at one end to catch cattle

lawless—not controlled by the law

native—originally from a specific place

petroglyphs—images scratched or chipped into rock; many petroglyphs tell stories of ancient peoples.

plains—large areas of flat land

plateau—an area of flat, raised land

reservation—an area of land the government has set aside for Native Americans

rodeos—events where people compete at tasks such as bull riding and calf roping; cowboys once completed these tasks as part of their daily work.

sacred—holy or having spiritual importance

service jobs—jobs that perform tasks for people or businesses

tourists—people who travel to visit another place

traditional—relating to a custom, idea, or belief handed down from one generation to the next

To Learn More

AT THE LIBRARY

Graham, Ian. *You Wouldn't Want to Work on the Hoover Dam!: An Explosive Job You'd Rather Not Do*. New York, N.Y.: Franklin Watts, 2012.

Lüsted, Marcia Amidon. *Nevada: The Silver State*. New York, N.Y.: PowerKids Press, 2011.

Roza, Greg. *Nevada: Past and Present*. New York, N.Y.: Rosen Central, 2011.

ON THE WEB

Learning more about Nevada is as easy as 1, 2, 3.

1. Go to www.factsurfer.com.

2. Enter "Nevada" into the search box.

3. Click the "Surf" button and you will see a list of related Web sites.

With factsurfer.com, finding more information is just a click away.

Index

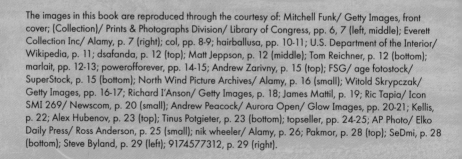